The River of Wealth:

HOW TO... BUILD UNIQUE STREAMS OF INCOME!

– BERKLEY M. BEAUMONT –

An environmentally friendly book printed and bound in England by www.printondemand-worldwide.com

This book is made entirely of chain-of-custody materials

www.fast-print.net/store.php

THE RIVER OF WEALTH:
HOW TO... BUILD UNIQUE STREAMS OF INCOME

A catalogue record for this book is available from the British Library

ISBN 978-178456-260-1

First published 2014 by
FASTPRINT PUBLISHING
Peterborough, England.

Table of Contents

Introduction

> ***Welcome to the River of Wealth!***

In this book we will teach you how to become wealthier. We cannot guarantee you will become super rich just by reading this book. You will also need to adapt and use what you learn here.

We are fairly certain though, that if you follow the advice in these pages, you are much more likely to become wealthier than if you had never read it. For the majority of people, the greatest sum of money they will earn will come from their regular salaried job over many years. **BUT DO NOT LET THAT STOP YOU** from becoming wealthier through what you read in this and similar books. It is one thing to read. It is another thing to act on what we have read. There are rivers of wealth flowing all around us, but we need the vision and commitments to be able to take advantage of them. *Are you ready to take a plunge in the river?*

> ***No one learned to swim, just standing by a river!***

Wealth is an attitude of mind, long before it becomes a product, service, or business process that helps meet the needs of a set of customers. This book will change your thoughts about wealth, the sources of wealth, the reasons for wealth, and the dangers of wealth as well as the blessings. This book will help you to have a mental and spiritual attitude of always seeing what the real needs are and how meeting those legitimate and legal needs can be profitable.

This book will take you further than you have probably gone before, in the journey of wealth creation; from dreams into the realities of making, and keeping or spending your wealth. Along the way, we shall discover some of the best principles of modern business, and we shall draw on ancient wellsprings of wisdom to inspire our journey.

> ***Are you ready for this? Then let's GO!***

Some basic thoughts

Envision a mighty river, not just a stream or a small creek, but a mighty river. Every river as a source and a destination. The river of wealth actually begins to flow within you before it flows outside you. The river of wealth begins by flowing out from you as ideas and business processes, but then it starts to flow to you bringing back wealth in returns!

Remember that it often takes several smaller streams to make the mighty river!

The river off your wealth should not just be about you. Along the way the river brings life to many places and people. The flow of your river of wealth should bring life to many others besides you. Rivers flow naturally from the source down towards the sea. Your business ideas need to be a natural fit to the market. Your business processes should cause wealth to flow naturally to you and from you into your lifestyle, which includes being a blessing to others in family, work and community. The destination of the river of your wealth should be greater, far greater than the source.

Rivers are fresh water. Your business ideas need to be fresh and new, or at least fresh and new ways of looking at existing problems. Keep you river clean, don't let is get filled with rubbish or polluted with hurtful material. Your river might live longer than you to be a blessing to generations to come. Keep it as fresh and pure as you can.

> ***Even mighty rivers begin as tiny sources!***

Some of the water in a river comes from rain that began as evaporation from the land and sea. This is called the hydrological cycle. Many business ideas are really not new, they spring out of the ideas that have evaporated up from the various surfaces we have travelled on in the journey of our life, and then form clouds of ideas in our minds and then fall into our life again as new ideas, combined droplets ***from a million sources of thoughts and influences, that we now do not even remember.***

Some river water has been trapped below ground seeping gradually through the rocks, like the ideas that have lain deep in the depths of our consciousness, seeping gradually through, sometimes only when disturbed or awakened by other ideas. Other water in a river comes from melting snow and ice, like those ideas that have remained frozen by the cold reception of rejection and ridicule, but which remain in our hearts until the season changes and warmer time, allow us to bring them into the light.

A river that stops flowing – is no longer a river!

But keep a sense of balance, because what is a big river for one, may be a stream to another. There are "rivers" in Europe that would only qualify as streams in parts of Africa and South

America where the mighty Nile, Congo and the Amazon flow! True success is always in being the best that you can be, not in trying to live someone else's life.

We shall return to these and other ideas in different forms as we journey together to make your business ideas into reality and help you create your river of wealth!

Chapter One –

How to Stand Strong!

Creating wealth is not an easy game. If that were the case, so many more would be swimming in wealth today. We should be realistic enough to agree at the start, that building your businesses will take some effort. So we will start by looking together at some of the secrets of strength for the journey. We will look at some basic things you will need to make you stronger, tougher and more determined than your competition!

> ***Wealth is an attitude of mind, long before it becomes a product, a service, or a business process.***

A Sound Mental Attitude

You should stay focussed on the prize

ahead. Champions win long before they win. Days, months and even years before the Olympic Winner stands on the podium with the flags waving in the breeze, with their national anthem playing and the weight of the medal on their neck; long before that ***THE ATHLETE HAD ALREADY SEEN THEMSELVES THERE!***

Do not wait until you succeed to see yourself as a success. **Past failures are not always an indication of future success,** but they can be key lessons in life. Your yesterdays are not necessarily part of your future. Don't wait until you win big to see yourself as a winner. The vison of that Olympic podium keeps the athlete going through many days, months and years of training. In today's world, you do not need years to build your business, but the

To be successful, we need to fill ourselves with success!

principles are the same.

Believe in Yourself!

Your thoughts are the source of your life. Believe in your Creator, the Almighty and believe in yourself! Believe that you were created not just to live well, but to cause others to live better as well. Believe that you have it in you, to do what it takes to be the best you can be! This not arrogance or pride, but a healthy and realistic attitude, that shows you have what it takes, to do what it takes, to be what it takes; to become who you are destined to be! This also means not being afraid to be tested, as every test is also an opportunity to become better, and ***to prove that you have what it takes to be better!*** Strong people

Are you interested? THEN READ ON!

are known by the tests they faced!

Remember, the benefits are worth the effort. Becoming wealthier enables you to be financially secure, but more than that; wealth allows you to BE! Increasing your wealth removes some of the pressure and allows you space to unfold and unfurl yourself from out of the constraints of everyday struggles of average life, into the freedom to discover and become yourself.

Believe in your Product!

Believe in your product. We shall talk more about product development and marketing a bit later, but it is really difficult to sell a product you do not believe in, and that includes YOURSELF! But just as much as you believe in yourself, you need to believe in your product. To believe in the product, you need to know that product better than anyone, because it is difficult to believe in something you do not know. Do not be afraid to test your product to the point where you can genuinely look anyone in the eyes and say to them "my product does what it says on the tin"!

That is the only way you can get enough people to believe in you enough, to listen to you enough, to buy your products enough; ***for you to become incredibly wealthy!*** Later on you can get other experts to work for you, but when you start out, you need to be the expert in your products.

> ***Becoming wealthier, is not and end in itself!***

Believe in Teamwork

You cannot travel this journey alone. Believe in your team. Value those who come into your business life. ***Many will***

have a capacity to enrich you and the business. Teams are not essential to every business situation. In fact there will be times when it is better to take the final decision alone. You also need to be strong enough to drop those who are becoming a negative influence. **When you need a team, pick a good one!** Sooner or later, you will need a team of people to help you. They may not all be part of the whole journey.

The team may be large or small. Some will only play their part briefly along the way. Some will play a much bigger role than others. Some may never work for you directly, but they are all useful! Even the ones who show you their negative side, have also played a useful role in helping you realise that not everyone will support

You reap what you sow!

your product or other ideas. Be big enough and strong enough to stay positive and to treat everyone who is part of your business journey with as much respect and courtesy as you can muster. ***Keep your eyes on the prize!***

Mental and Spiritual Attitude

A healthy mental attitude also comes from having a good "spiritual attitude". That means taking time to be in tune with a true source of real wisdom. It means understanding that there is a bigger picture to existence, which helps you to see the bigger picture in your own life and business. ***Wealth requires discipline!***

For a source of refreshing daily wisdom, try the Holy Bible. The Bible, is a collection of books that includes poetry, history, wisdom and of course religious doctrine. The wisdom books in the Bible include the Books of Job and Proverbs, Ecclesiastes, Psalms and the Song of Songs. They are well worth a read, if only because the wisdom found there, is from a different and more Eastern root than the Greco-Roman-Renaissance logic of Western Europe. If you want a different and sometimes quite radical perspective on life, try the Bible! For a start, try browsing a chapter of the Book of Proverbs each day. Just find quiet moments at the start and end of the day, but also in between things. ***Just for a couple of minutes, tune out to the world and tune your inner self into the ancient wisdom in this wonderful book...***

You need to feed and refresh your inner self!

What is Wisdom?

Wisdom is the ability to apply knowledge successfully (or correctly) to situations. Having the wisdom to apply the knowledge you have, will often be more important than how much knowledge you have! There are many who have a great deal of knowledge gained perhaps from attending formal education or training and are experts in that field, but are not known for great wisdom in other areas of their life.

Healthier, wealthier living is spiritual and mental, as well as physical

As a young student many years ago, I remember we once had a mathematics teacher who was absolutely brilliant at solving equations, and would fill the blackboard with his mathematical genius. Yet he seemed to walk around in an absent minded haze, with his hair and clothing in "disarray"; looking (and occasionally smelling) like a relative of Worzel

Gummidge, who had just escaped from a rubbish tip!

Wisdom includes being wise about your work life balance, and taking reasonable care of your health. You need to be wise enough, to stay healthy enough, to work hard enough to increase your wealth, and then live long enough to enjoy it! So it is wisdom to get as fit as you can, and most people can do ***at least something*** to improve their fitness. Do you have an exercise program?

Physical Fitness

Add a good fitness plan to your exercise program, which includes eating a balanced diet and keeping track of your progress. You will probably lose some weight and gain in fitness and energy levels, and mental concentration among other things. Remember to have a talk with a doctor or other medical specialists about any possible health issues you may have. That is wisdom too. Making exercise a regular part of your new healthy lifestyle is a wise investment in your future.

Chapter Two

How to Turn Needs into Wealth

Having many business ideas, even very good business ideas will not necessarily increase your wealth. The real secret lies in firstly being able to know which ideas will actually sell and make you money, and secondly finding the right way to implement your idea. *You are in the right book!*

> ***To understand the market, you must identify the need!***

One Good Idea!

Just one idea making you money in a growing marketplace, is worth a thousand ideas still sitting around in your head, or gathering dust on a shelf. It has been said, you do not need to reinvent the mousetrap. You can simply make a better one, or just be better at selling the mousetraps that already exist. ***But you need a real product that will meet real needs in a real market,*** and that will make real money flow to you! Your product should meet real needs of real people who feel that need enough to part with some real money; and ***for long enough for you to make as big a pile of beautiful profit as possible!***

The real needs should be felt by real customers. Needs in your own life can point to a product that others will pay for, **BUT WHO?** You need to know who your customers are. What is making them "tick"? What do they want? How can your business help them? What product will they be willing to pay a particular price for? Apart from the customers, the next most important group, are other business people in the same or related product field as you. *In other words, what (or who) is the competition?* You also need to be realistic about risks and other possible problems such as regulations that affect your business.

Stand out From the Crowd

Know your product, your market AND your customers!

Think of how you can make your product (or service) different or better than what other businesses provide. Presentation and service can be as important as the product itself. Excellence in products and services is actually good business sense.

If excellence marks you out above others in the market, ***it can eventually led to significantly increased wealth.***

Later in this book, we will look at the balance between time, cost and quality.

You do not always have to do something new, just finding a new way to do something better, can increase your wealth. Your business idea does not even have to be particularly high-tech. ***There are existing products, even very old products that are still selling extremely well!***

For example, the Holy Bible is the best-selling book of all time! The Guinness Book of Records states that between 1815 and 1975, ***about 5 billion copies were sold***. Each year, the Bible still outsells other books around the globe. Electronic versions of the Bible for use on mobile devices, are now becoming extremely popular all over the world. If

If you are not making money, you are losing money!

you can find some people who still need to buy Bibles, or if you can produce the latest and best Bible smartphone app, you can become very rich just doing that! So old products still sell!

Test Your Business Ideas

Setting up your Internet business is now easier than ever before, but you need to test your business ideas. One of the first tests for your business idea, is to find out what is already in the market. With the Internet now available to so many people, searching for products online is easier than ever before. You should look out for products that do the same or similar to you own idea, even if they are differently named. Find out how that works and what you can learn from them. ***If you can't beat them, do you need to join them?***

If a similar product or idea exists in your own immediate area, ***can you get a slice of that action?*** Sometimes a small piece of a big pie that has already been baked, is better than baking your own from scratch. ***Is there a similar product in another market that you can introduce more locally?***

SWOT Analysis

You can also do a SWOT Analysis (or SWOT Matrix) for your product and for your business. Each heading in the list below will give you part of the picture of your business or product. Putting the answers to each of these headings together will build the overall picture and help you to know

> ***It is usually more profitable to be part of a solution, than part of a problem!***

what to keep, and what to improve or to leave out. You can even use it to evaluate yourself! SWOT stands for:

- **Strengths**
- **Weaknesses**
- **Opportunities**
- **Threats**

Have a solution mindset! Treat ALL the information that you receive as possible sources of ideas for creating or improving your business. Keep a notebook where you write business ideas down for further evaluation. The majority of these may never see the light of day, ***but just one could become your river of wealth!*** Use these kinds of deliberate habits to keep your mind fresh and focussed on innovation.

You and your business should develop together!

Feed your mind

Feed your mind with other useful information in the area of the business idea you are trying to implement. Read books, watch videos, listen to CDs by those who have expertise in this or related fields. Your human mind is more powerful that any computer available to you. But ***like a computer, the mind is only as good as the information put into it, and the person using it!***

Every business you develop also will develop you in some way. It has been said that ***you cannot develop a business more than you are willing to develop yourself!*** Have an attitude of life-long learning. Take courses, go to seminars. Join us on our weekly Internet

> ***A life that stops learning, has stopped living!***

classes. For just a small fee each month, you can be part of a group of like-minded people who are increasing their worth and increasing their wealth. ***Life itself is a learning curve.*** Rediscover a child-like sense of wonder and curiosity. Make each day, a day of discovery. Most things that are found, are found by someone who is looking for them!

Study the Market

Understand your market. Do not shy away from data and statistics. They are the "bread and butter" of business life. Learn to love the figures that tell you more about your business. Make these figures your best friends. ***They will save you money and help you build your river of wealth.***

> ***Business research is a good investment!***

There are many sources of data and statistics out there to help you understand the market in which your business operates. Many people use the terms Data and statistics as if they are the same. Data is the information gathered from the surveys. Statistics are the summarised analysis of the raw data.

Time spent studying the market is a good investment and will repay itself in helping you get your business right. Remember we said that your business should fit "naturally" into the environment. Just like a river that flows along the easiest possible route, your business needs to fit with the contours of the market.

Sometimes it might seem that new products or businesses have changed the market, but if you look more closely, you find that the conditions for the new product or business were already there.

It is just that no one saw the opportunity (or had the capacity to exploit the opportunity) except that one special person (or group) who were on the lookout!

Study Relevant Policies and Demographics

> ***Statistics can be boring, but they can also make you money!***

It is important to at least be aware of government policies, and the relevant laws and regulations around your business area. That can also be boring but it is better than investing, only to find that your way is blocked by some new trading laws for example. There are usually several government websites with very useful information for the new business start-up.

Demographic surveys (including census data) that give you breakdowns of people by age, gender, employment, income, ethnicity and culture etc. are also very useful to the serious entrepreneur. There are also reports on consumer statistics that help you see patterns of preferences in the way people are spending their money, and then you can see more clearly ***how to make some of that money flow to you!***

> ***Watch where the market moves to see where you can make more money!***

Keep an eye on the overall economy and the various economic trends, not just in your immediate market, but also in other markets that can have an impact on yours. There will be short term and longer term trends in several areas of the economy. ***Be aware that downturns in***

the economy can also be opportunities to make money!

In times of recession, people need to save money, and so new cheaper ways of doing things become more attractive. People that have been in a market longer than you have much of their operations fixed and may find it difficult to be flexible enough to meet the change required. ***That can be your opportunity!***

Always keep looking for the needs that your business ideas can meet, whether among people that you know and perhaps work with, or more widely in society.

Feedback is Important

Stay connected to people who help push you towards your goals. Interactions with others are a valuable source of refinement for your ideas. But be your own best critic when it comes to business ideas. Ruthlessly evaluate them for their real potential to make you some real money. ***It may be that only very few ideas you have will make it to profitability in the marketplace***, but having the mind set of an innovator is a big step towards increasing your wealth.

Customer feedback is like gold dust. Customer responses can modify your delivery processes or help you create new products that can serious increase your wealth! Social media empowers the customer to interact with business in new and innovative ways.

The same social media also empowers you to get massive amounts of useful information from customers, in ways that business in years gone by could only have dreamed of. This allows you make your customers a real part of the business. They then feel that they are being taken seriously and that you are responding to their needs. Your customers can then become your main focus group, and they can be your main consultants in developing your company and your products.

Customer feedback is like gold dust.

Chapter Three
How to Develop Your Products

Development of new products includes all the processes involved in the design and creation (prototyping and testing) of the new product or service, as well as the marketing of that product. Ideally you need a real identifiable product that meets the needs of paying customers, in an expanding market.

In the previous chapter, we looked mainly at identifying the market opportunity (need). In this chapter, we are looking more at how we develop the idea of how to meet that need, into a viable product.

ARE YOU READY TO PUSH FURTHER? THEN PLEASE READ ON!

Time Cost and Quality

Most customer needs are met by products in one of three areas (or combinations of these):

1. **Time**
2. **Cost**
3. **Quality**

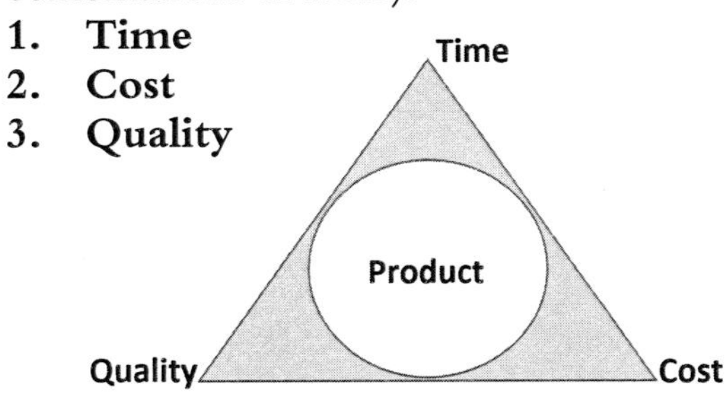

The Time, Cost, Quality Product Framework

> ***Product Development is strategic, like building an army!***

Businesses must produce products or services that meet customer needs in a timely manner, within production costs and to the right, or acceptable quality. In the same way, the best products or services are those which save customers time, deliver or enhance quality of life or business, and are seen as good value at that price (cost). The exception to this rule could be the high end luxury market where cost is itself a status symbol, and production time is also as long as it takes, because the highest quality is the most desirable.

Generally speaking, these three factors of time, cost and quality (above) will help determine the best products for any market. The products will then have to be launched, distributed and supported, along with revenues being collected. We will talk in more detail about marketing your product in a later chapter. ***Have you started thinking through your products?***

> ***Almost all products and services are governed by these same factors!***

By now you should start having some good ideas about:

- **What market you are entering and why**
- **What's the state of the economy you are in**
- **What's the state of the sector you are targeting**
- **What real need you can meet**
- **Who would be "hungry" for your products**
- **What price they might pay**
- **What is the competition and**
- **What product you can offer within time cost and quality?**

Stay ahead of the game by asking ***what, why, where, when, how and what next questions.*** Keep updating or refreshing your products, and also introduce new

Always ask, "What should happen next?"

products from time to time, to keep your old customers engaged and to keep expanding your market. So as soon as you have put one product out, you need to be thinking about the follow-up.

Aiming for variations on a product already in the market means that you spend less in telling people what your product does. This carries a lower, ***more acceptable level of risk.*** You might have noticed that some road cyclists like to ride behind others. The rider in front does the work of pushing the air apart to get through. Those behind have less to do as they "ride in the slipstream". This is also a good business tactic, for smaller firms or startups. Although a minority of smaller businesses do bring totally new products to market, most find it easier to enter existing product areas until they have grown stronger.

A mix of products will support your income better. Eventually, you should be aiming to have a mix of income streams, including some stocks and shares. You may notice that you have some products that sell less regularly, but still bring in a good profit when they do sell. **You need to mix these with other products that sell much more frequently.**

You may decide to have some permanent products that are always on your website, and that long term customers are familiar with. They have known and loved and trusted these products over time. Other products may be temporary or more seasonal. However, ***temporary products can become more permanent.*** Other products may fit with various regions, religions, cultures and ethnicities. Other niche products may serve other particular groups of customers, who may be a small group, but who are loyal and buy regularly.

Finally, you need some products that just help open the market and bring customers through the shop door (or website). This last group of products may sometimes be sold at a small loss, in order to gain entry to the market (share) and ***are sometimes called "loss leaders".*** Remember that no product lasts forever. Eventually, even the best product range will have to be refreshed, replaced, or dropped altogether. This is referred to as the "Product Cycle".

A mix of products will support your income better

Sketch it out and Kick it About

The first part of product design is purely conceptual. Think the product through, sketch it out, and kick the idea about. You can try it on family and friends and possibly use a group of friends or gather a group online. This is relatively easy to do by ***advertising a small free gift in return for participating in a small trial run*** of an idea similar to yours (not the actual idea). This allows you to refine your idea and iron out some of the kinks. You need to be realistic about how the product or service will meet the needs of others, unless you are designing it completely for yourself! Once you have a very clear idea about what works, you will be ready to try the market. Especially with manufactured goods, test before you invest in production, with a trial run.

Chapter Four

How to Brand Your Products

The purpose of branding is to make people recognise (and choose) your products and services. ***Try to integrate the visual with the colour-scheme and the sound of the name*** in some ways to make them a complete whole. It helps if fairly early in the design of your product, you are already thinking about how you will present it to buyers. You may find that having a brand concept, even if that is only a draft, will help you with the rest of the design of the product. There are a number of websites now where ***you can buy logos online at relatively cheap prices,*** and you are then free to own and download them, and adapt them to suit your purpose. Remember ***you need to***

stand out from the crowd of other products and services out there. Here are some examples of types of branding that you can get some ideas from.

Kinds of Branding

Product branding seeks to get people to buy one product over another. This is common in supermarkets. **Personal (or individual) branding** is used by people who already have a well-known public profile. ***Professional athletes and people in show business would be examples of personal branding.*** Well-known brands will sometimes bring a high profile "star" to identify with their product. This is more of product or

> ***Branding is meant to get your products and services noticed and chosen over others!***

brand endorsement, and sponsorship of the athlete by the brand, in order to achieve higher visibility.

Corporate branding is meant to identify the whole ethos of the company as well as what it sells. This type of branding is applied across the corporation, on cars and other vehicles as well as on official staff clothing and PR items like give-away pens etc. Because the corporate brand is so identified with all aspects of the company, it can also be very vulnerable to the reputation of the company, for example if there is a corporate scandal. In such cases we say that the brand has been tarnished.

Your brand(s) will be associated with the good AND the bad of your business!

Some branding is regional or identifies with a particular city. Think of sports teams and some government agencies, and also some large entities like power or transport companies. You may also find some examples of ethnic or cultural branding as when products and services are identified with a group of people or their culture. There are many other sub-variants of brands, including environmental brands and luxury brands etc. and sometimes a brand can fall into more than one category. *What kind of brand have you given your product or service?*

Chapter Five

How to Market Your Products on the Internet

Setting up a website and an online shop is now quite easy and we do not need to dwell much on that here. It is the promotion that often ***makes the difference in how you stand out from the crowd!*** Promotion is all about how you present your products and services to the market and to the customers or clients. Promotion is part of marketing. Even product development could be seen as part of marketing. In some ways aspects of the whole process we have outlined in this book could be called "various phases of marketing". But for our purposes here, we have split them up. In this chapter we will bring a few things together, and concentrate more on

Internet marketing with a focus on Internet advertising and sales. It is however better to use a mix of marketing methods that works for you.

The "5 Ps" of marketing are Product, Price, Place and Promotion

Product	The right product "fit" for the right market, that will attract the right customer
Price	The right price that the customer will happily pay for the value of the purchase.
Place	The right place (physical or online location) easily accessible to the customer and easy for them to use.
Promotion	The final stage of marketing. The invitation to consumers or clients to engage with the products and services on offer.

Brand recognition (awareness) is key to much of your promotional effort, especially your advertising and sales strategy. Many people starting out in business spend far too much money on

Price is what you sell at. Value is what it means to the buyer!

advertising that does not bring them any returns.

Online Advertising

Make your online advertising as simple and direct as possible and ***make sure the online advert takes those who click on it, straight through to products they can buy.*** Build the adverts and your shopping pages to grab IMMEDIATE attention. People who come to your page should ***IMMEDIATELY BE AWARE OF THE BENEFITS OF BUYING FROM YOU!***

In business, your reputation is everything!

Use plenty of testimonials from previous happy customers in your online advertising. Always give ***a simple***

money back guarantee for what you sell, and you will sell much more. From the first visit to your website, people should ***immediately be leaving you their contact details and helping you evaluate the products and services*** you sell to them.

Make it attractive for visitors to your website to give you ***as much information as possible,*** in return for a free gift or a discount. That will also enable you to ***follow them up for a repeat sale***, and their feedback should also help you give them ***better products to buy in the future.***

Add on some other products into your online shop to make it more attractive. These other products might not be made by you, but they should be related to your own products in some way. This will add more value to your shop. ***You can also add value for people who visit your site by offering them a newsletter,*** with industry tips and updates for free.

You can also rebrand some digital and other products under license, and sell them from your website under your own brand, but always check the license. Remember your "front end products" are always cheaper. They are just there to help you sell your "back end products" which are more expensive. ***You can also have several websites with different names, but basically the same products.*** That can also help increase your online sales.

Direct mail (and direct email) are still good ways to build up your client base. You can still buy legitimate lists online, but let the buyer beware! In all your marketing, you are looking for people with legitimate needs, who are hungry for solutions. You can also look at partnering with, or using other industries that have clients who might be interested in your products (and who may have disposable cash). If you sell umbrellas or leather briefcases, you should know all the golf clubs in town!

How to use Google and Facebook

Many people think that Facebook and Google are the best ways to get new clients but both have their problems. With Facebook, it is hard to convert "likes" and "friends" into viable paying clients. So you can spend time and money building up your Facebook pages, and find that it has had little impact on your sales. You should ***use Facebook more as an "advertising sign"*** to draw people to the website and get them into your shop. So being on Facebook can be useful, but it is not an end in itself. Use your investment of time and money on Facebook wisely, and it will pay you back.

With Google, it is better to use pay-per-click than pay per view. With clicks, you can bring people through to your landing page immediately. Your purpose should be to get them into your shop and to start buying front end products immediately! If your website is designed to show people an immediate benefit, you are more likely to generate sales from pay-per-click.

Facebook Friends and Google Ad Viewers are NOT all paying customer!

Interactive marketing

Never stop studying your market and your customers. As you learn more about them, offer them premium (back end) products that are more tailored to their needs, and that bring you a better return. Refresh your website and products from time to time as outlined earlier above.

All of ***these are ways you outflank and overtake the competition.*** Remember that you do not just want sales, you want repeat sales. You want to build long lasting and profitable relationships with happy satisfied customers. Word of mouth recommendations by your customers to their friends and family ***will always be your best advertising, and it is generally free!***

The great thing about online selling is that you do not need to hold stock. A number of "Fulfilment Houses" now exist who will take care of all that and more for you, including:

- **Storage of Goods**
- **Handling of Orders**
- **Picking and packing**
- **Shipping**
- **Handling Returns**

Build your product promotion into a community of interest!

You can find several of these fulfilment houses online by using a search engine. They will do the heavy lifting for you ***and you can kick back and relax while the river of wealth just keeps on flowing!*** They will also send you Management Reports.

The new social media allows you to do a new kind of "interactive marketing", where you ***engage with customers in a more informal way*** and they feel very much a part of your business and the products and services that you sell. Digital systems and social media in particular can help

Let your customers tell you the products and services they want to buy from you.

you ***give the individual consumer that feeling or personal care and attention*** in ways that were not possible before now. You can respond to individual email messages and online postings directly, or even have automated replies. As we have noted earlier, the feedback you get from such interactions can help you improve your services.

If you listen to your customers, they can help you grow your business!

By now the ideas you had for products and services should have taken shape. Read through the instructions in this book again and again.

- Look for sales and repeat sales, as well as personal data and demographic information for future sales
- Automate (and possibly replicate) the processes so that you can sit back and enjoy this river of wealth.

- Build one stream, and let it begin to flow, then build another and another, till you have ***A RIVER OF WEALTH!***

You do not need to just keep creating more jobs for yourself to do. That will eventually wear you out! You goal should be to see each stream of wealth grow from a trickle to where it flows naturally in the environment with minimal intervention from you.

Then you can move on to building the next stream. The boundaries between projects are not fixed and sometimes they may overlap.

Chapter Six

How to Enjoy Your Wealth

Someone once said that the drive to improve your life and become rich is a mental illness, to which they got the reply ***"If richness is a sickness, I want to get infected right now"!***

Always believe you can become wealthier than you are. You do not have to be a genius to become wealthy. In fact fewer people with extremely high IQ actually become very wealthy. IQ is important at the lower end of the spectrum of wealth, but the higher you go, the less important a high IQ becomes. Intelligence is no guarantee that you will have ***the personal and financial discipline to get and control large sums of money.***

Education is also no guarantee of wealth. Many of the top business people do not even have a formal education. So always believe that you can become wealthier than you are. Just follow the guides in this book and you will be able to create income streams that eventually add up to a river of wealth in your life.

Work Life Balance

> ***Wealth needs discipline rather than education or intelligence!***

Work life balance is important so that you don't just get richer, but you actually enjoy it! Can you be rich and unhappy? Absolutely, otherwise there would be no divorces, drug addiction or suicides among the stars of Hollywood. But, ***it is also quite possible to be wealthy and also live a happy, balanced and***

satisfied life. Work life balance is bringing stability between your work and the rest of your life

Balance?

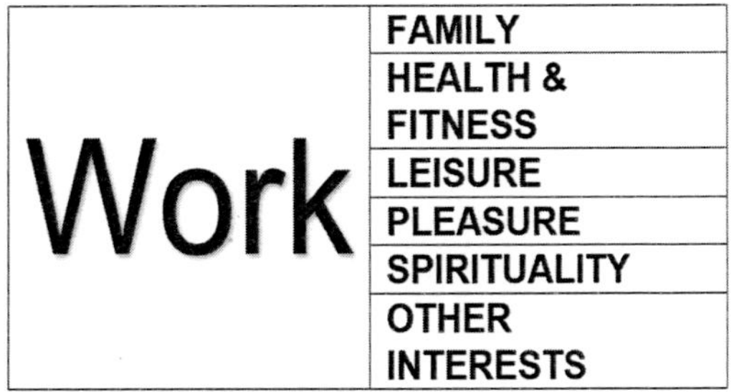

Meet the Silent Rich!

> ***Keep balance between your work and your life!***

Only a minority of wealthy people actually live the flashy life that we might imagine. Many of the truly wealthy people live quite modestly, and ***often, people who know them do not even know that they are super rich!***

These "silent rich" use fairly "normal" homes and cars and often do not even travel "first class". They are careful with their money and that is one reason w***hy they have not only become rich, but they tend to stay rich!*** These are often the wealthy who have discovered the secret to happiness and ***they do not let their wealth interfere with their happiness.***

They stick to a life that they can control and they still do the simple things that they know will give them real joy, rather than pursuing "off the shelf" happiness, which they might never find. These are the rich who have found certain activities in and outside work that they can do well, and be happy doing. They are also quite well informed about issues such as health and fitness. They know what investments they can follow without the stress of too much risk. Getting and keeping wealth is a lifetime task as well as a lifestyle choice.

Be Healthy, Wealthy and WISE

> ***Getting and keeping wealth is a lifetime task as well as a lifestyle choice***

Decide on what you can change for the better that will bring greater balance into your life. ***Be realistic about yourself what you can keep control of and what you really need to avoid.*** Set some priorities that you can keep without compromising. Keep focussed on a few things that help you stay balanced and in control of your life

Enjoy your life. Take charge of your surroundings. As you become able to afford more, do not let the surroundings control you. Have a number of simple activities or hobbies that give you pleasure, plant flowers in your garden. Play with the grandchildren. Go and listen to an orchestra. Keep a small network of other balanced and happy people that remain in your business and personal life, over a relatively long period of time. Take care of your health and fitness, but don't make them the gods in your life

Care for your body soul and spirit. Take time to join a good church and worship God in a refreshing atmosphere, where it is not about how much money you give to the church… Love and worship God, Love and respect yourself and your family and friends. Love and respect your neighbours. Love and respect the river of wealth that flows to you. Treat it well and it will take care of you and whoever you leave it to. At the same time, find ways to cut off and cut out the things (and sometime staff and colleagues) that do not fit in this plan.

Be generous to those who work with and for you. Give to the poor and the needy when and how you can. Let the river of wealth you have been blessed with be a blessing to others.

Stay thankful, stay grateful – life could be worse!

ENJOY YOUR RIVER OF LIFE!

To contact the author,
Or to join any of our wealth creation,
Strategic Management
Or personal (and spiritual)
development programmes
Please email:
consultant@mindstrategies.co.uk.

ND - #0267 - 080726 - C0 - 148/105/6 - PB - 9781784562601 - Gloss Lamination